LOOKING INTO THE PAST:
PEOPLE, PLACES, AND CUSTOMS

Ancient and Annual Customs

by

Dwayne E. Pickels

Chelsea House Publishers

CHELSEA HOUSE PUBLISHERS

Editor in Chief Stephen Reginald
Managing Editor James D. Gallagher
Production Manager Pamela Loos
Art Director Sara Davis
Picture Editor Judy Hasday
Senior Production Editor Lisa Chippendale
Designers Takeshi Takahashi, Keith Trego

3 5 7 9 8 6 4 2

Library of Congress Cataloging-in-Publication Data

Pickels, Dwayne E.
Ancient and annual customs / by Dwayne E. Pickels.

   p. cm. — (Looking into the past)
Includes bibliographical references and index.
Summary: Describes various ancient customs and traditions,
such as the ducking stool, the maypole, and calling the
hours, as well as the historic roots of holiday celebrations
still followed.

ISBN 0-7910-4682-6
1. Holidays—History—Juvenile literature. 2. Manners and
customs—Juvenile literature. [1. Holidays—History. 2.
Manners and customs.] I. Title. II. Series.
GT3933.P52 1997   97-28788
394.26—dc21   CIP
                                    AC

CONTENTS

CULTURE, CUSTOMS, AND RITUALS

The important moments of our lives—from birth through puberty, aging, and death—are made more meaningful by culture, customs, and rituals. But what is culture? The word *culture,* broadly defined, includes the way of life of an entire society. This encompasses customs, rituals, codes of manners, dress, languages, norms of behavior, and systems of beliefs. Individuals are both acted on by and react to a culture—and so generate new cultural forms and customs.

What is custom? Custom refers to accepted social practices that separate one cultural group from another. Every culture contains basic customs, often known as rites of transition or passage. These rites, or ceremonies, occur at different stages of life, from birth to death, and are sometimes religious in nature. In all cultures of the world today, a new baby is greeted and welcomed into its family through ceremony. Some ceremonies, such as the bar mitzvah, a religious initiation for teenage Jewish boys, mark the transition from childhood to adulthood. Marriage also is usually celebrated by a ritual of some sort. Death is another rite of transition. All known cultures contain beliefs about life after death, and all observe funeral rites and mourning customs.

What is a ritual? What is a rite? These terms are used interchangeably to describe a ceremony associated with a custom. The English ritual of shaking hands in greeting, for example, has become part of that culture. The washing of one's hands could be considered a ritual which helps a person achieve an accepted level of cleanliness—a requirement of the cultural beliefs that person holds.

The books in this series, *Looking into the Past: People,*

Places, and Customs, explore many of the most interesting rituals of different cultures through time. For example, did you know that in the year A.D. 1075 William the Conqueror ordered that a "Couvre feu" bell be rung at sunset in each town and city of England, as a signal to put out all fires? Because homes were made of wood and had thatched roofs, the bell served as a precaution against house fires. Today, this custom is no longer observed as it was 900 years ago, but the modern word *curfew* derives from its practice.

Another ritual that dates from centuries long past is the Japanese Samurai Festival. This colorful celebration commemorates the feats of the ancient samurai warriors who ruled the country hundreds of years ago. Japanese citizens dress in costumes, and direct descendants of warriors wear samurai swords during the festival. The making of these swords actually is a separate religious rite in itself.

Different cultures develop different customs. For example, people of different nations have developed various interesting ways to greet each other. In China 100 years ago, the ordinary salutation was a ceremonious, but not deep, bow, with the greeting "Kin t'ien ni hao ma?" (Are you well today?). During the same era, citizens of the Indian Ocean island nation Ceylon (now called Sri Lanka) greeted each other by placing their palms together with the fingers extended. When greeting a person of higher social rank, the hands were held in front of the forehead and the head was inclined.

Some symbols and rituals rooted in ancient beliefs are common to several cultures. For example, in China, Japan, and many of the countries of the East, a tortoise is a symbol of protection from black magic, while fish have represented fertility, new life, and prosperity since the beginnings of human civilization. Other ancient fertility symbols have been incorporated into religions we still practice today, and so these ancient beliefs remain a part of our civilization. A more recent belief, the legend of Santa Claus, is the story of a kind benefactor who brings gifts to the good children of the world. This story appears in the lore of nearly every nation. Each country developed its own variation on the legend and each celebrates Santa's arrival in a different way.

New rituals are being created all the time. On April 21, 1997, for example, the cremated remains of 24 people were launched into orbit around Earth on a Pegasus rocket. Included among the group whose ashes now head toward their "final frontier" are Gene Roddenberry, creator of the television series *Star Trek,* and Timothy Leary, a countercultural icon of the 1960s. Each person's remains were placed in a separate aluminum capsule engraved with the person's name and a commemorative phrase. The remains will orbit the Earth every 90 minutes for two to ten years. When the rocket does re-enter Earth's atmosphere, it will burn up with a great burst of light. This first-time ritual could become an accepted rite of passage, a custom in our culture that would supplant the current ceremonies marking the transition between life and death.

Curiosity about different customs, rites, and rituals dates back to the mercantile Greeks of classical times. Herodotus (484–425 B.C.), known as the "Father of History," described Egyptian culture. The Roman historian Tacitus (A.D. 55–117) similarly wrote a lengthy account about the customs of the "modern" European barbarians. From the Greeks to Marco Polo, from Columbus to the Pacific voyages of Captain James Cook, cultural differences have fascinated the literate world. The books in the *Looking into the Past* series collect the most interesting customs from many cultures of the past and explain their origins, meanings, and relationship to the present day.

In the future, space travel may very well provide the impetus for new cultures, customs, and rituals, which will in turn enthrall and interest the peoples of future millennia.

Fred L. Israel
The City College of the City University of New York

CONTRIBUTORS

Senior Consulting Editor FRED L. ISRAEL is an award-winning historian. He received the Scribe's Award from the American Bar Association for his work on the Chelsea House series *The Justices of the United States Supreme Court.* A specialist in early American history, he was general editor for Chelsea's *1897 Sears Roebuck Catalog.* Dr. Israel has also worked in association with Dr. Arthur M. Schlesinger, jr. on many projects, including *The History of U.S. Presidential Elections* and *The History of U.S. Political Parties.* They are currently working together on the Chelsea House series *The World 100 Years Ago,* which looks at the traditions, customs, and cultures of many nations at the turn of the century.

DWAYNE E. PICKELS is an award-winning reporter with the *Greensburg (Pa.) Tribune-Review.* A Magna Cum Laude graduate of the University of Pittsburgh, where he cofounded the literary magazine *Pendulum,* Dwayne won a Pennsylvania Newspaper Publishers' Association (PNPA) Keystone Press Award in 1992. He currently resides in Scottdale, Pa., with his wife, Mary, and their daughter, Kaidia Leigh. In his free time, he is currently immersed in a number of literary pursuits—which include a novel based on Celtic myth and legend. In addition to writing, Dwayne enjoys outdoor excursions, including bird watching, hiking, photography, and target shooting . . . along with typically futile attempts at fishing.

OVERVIEW

Ancient and Annual Customs

H

ave you ever wondered why we celebrate Halloween at the end of October, or why we send brightly colored cards and gifts to our sweethearts in February? Why did some of our ancestors dance around ribbon-laced trees in May and haul special logs from the forest to burn in December? These are only some of the ancient and annual customs that, over the years, have been woven into the intricate fabric of Western society.

Most of the traditions examined in this book hail from the British Isles, primarily England. While many originated in medieval times, some date back even earlier, to the pagan cultures that florished in Britain centuries before the birth of Christ. The coming of Christianity signaled great changes in the way of life of these peoples, but many of their traditions weren't abandoned so much as adapted to fit a Christian framework.

Some of the customs described here were rooted in practicality, such as "Archery on the Green" or "the Curfew Bell." And some—like "the Midsummer Eve Bonfire"—followed seasonal events. Still others, such as "the Lord of Misrule" and "the Mummers," were pure flights of fancy, designed, it would seem, mainly as an excuse to celebrate. Other "odd" customs described in this book related to protection, punishment, love, charity, laughter, pain, music, death, health, comfort, security and even a nice hot cup of tea—the basic ingredients of human existence.

So maybe they weren't so far-fetched after all.

Nonetheless, while a few of these practices and beliefs have lingered on virtually intact into the modern age, others have changed greatly, and some have been nearly forgotten. A closer look at these ancient customs offers a fascinating glimpse at a bygone world.

THE YULE LOG

uring ancient times, fire played a crucial role in day-to-day life. After all, until technology advanced enough to provide more efficient means of manufacturing life-sustaining heat, it was fire that kept people alive half the year or more in many parts of the world.

So it's only natural that fire would play an equally prominent role in the customs that arose from ancient times—especially those customs that corresponded with winter. One such tradition was finding and transporting home the Yule log.

The word *yule* is said to claim its ancestry from the Old English word *geol*, originally one of the names of a pre-Christian (pagan) midwinter festival. In later years, as did many other aspects of pagan society, the word found its way into Christian applications. In this case, it became closely associated with the Christmas season.

The Yule Log.

A medieval observance accompanied by great mirth and revelry, the Yule log custom—a search for a special piece of wood—has a modern counterpart in the annual quest for just the right Christmas tree, a tradition fondly observed by many families. Once it was secured, the Yule log was always kindled from a portion of the charred remains of the log left over from the previous year's celebration. In fact, it was an old superstition that "the evil one" could do no mischief in a house in which the remains of the Yule log were preserved from year to year.

Most importantly, once the sacred fire was lit, it had to be carefully maintained until New Year. To many superstitious people, it was a bad omen if the hearth was allowed to grow cold.

Hallowe'en

ne of the few pagan-rooted traditions still observed today, Hallowe'en is derived from the ancient pagan festival of Samhain (pronounced Sah-win). With Christianity's rise in pagan Celtic nations, the custom was adapted into a vigil for the feast of All Saints' Day (November 1) and observed on October 31, otherwise known as All Hallows' Eve—thus the modern word, *Halloween*.

Nonetheless, it was believed that on this night the veil that separates the world of mortals and the normally inaccessible "Otherworld" became thin or disappeared completely. This allowed the inhabitants of that dimension—spirits of the dead and the magical faeries (also known as the *sidhe*)—to freely enter the world of the living.

On this perilous night, Celtic peoples of the British Isles lit bonfires to keep these malevolent spirit visitors at bay. But with the Celtic love of a good time, they also spent the

evening immersed in merriment, enjoying a variety of sports and games. Fortune telling and other divinations of the future were also practiced. Many people—engaging in a custom that came to be known as "the guisers"—would don disguises resembling all manner of supernatural hosts and masquerade around the villages to confuse the spirits, which evolved into the modern tradition of trick or treat.

On a more somber note, the festival of Samhain marked the end of summer and the beginning of the dark half of the year, winter. In fact, some sources indicate that the Celts began their year at this time, making November 1 a sort of New Year's Day. That they may have started the year with darkness lends credence to the theory that Celts also began their days at dusk, instead of dawn—leading Julius Caesar to call them "the people of the night."

THE CURFEW BELL

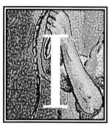ntroduction of the curfew bell into English tradition is credited to William I, who lived from around 1027 to 1087. Better known as William the Conqueror, he was named duke of Normandy in 1035 and became the first Norman king of England in 1066, after emerging victorious from the Battle of Hastings. By 1071, he had successfully quelled all opposition.

William the Conqueror has been described by some as a harsh but practical ruler who created a strong feudal order in England through the construction of castles and realignment of the country's military and land-holding systems. A minor but interesting example of a "harsh but practical" rule the Norman king instituted during his reign was the customary ringing of the curfew bell.

The curfew bell chimed at sunset during summer months and at eight o'clock during the winter season. It was a strict signal that meant "extinguish all fires." However, it is

said that this was not as much an act of Norman tyranny as it was a necessary safety precaution against fire in a time when houses were chiefly constructed of dry wood with straw roofs—prime kindling material.

William's decree may well have been one of the earliest lessons in fire safety, as unattended fires in such conditions could have proven disastrous in an era that had never heard of a fire department. In apparent acceptance of the wisdom of the mandate, the custom of the curfew bell is said to have carried on long after his rule in some parts of England.

THE MUMMERS

The mummers—traveling bands of performers—are said to have made frequent appearances at royal and wealthy courts, country houses, and various other places in England during the Middle Ages. And these early theater troupes were reportedly open to people of all ranks, male and female.

Though they are said to have included some elements of song and dance, the mummers' plays were very dramatic and often revealed an interest in the timeless themes of death and renewal. Additionally, numerous shapes and forms of animals were represented in garish makeup and lavish costumes, as were other characters—such as St. George and the Dragon. In fact, a variation of the legendary hero, known as "Green George," was a popular central figure in many mummers' productions, said to have symbolized the essence of spring in winter.

The grand pageants and processions with which the citi-

The Mummers 654

zens of medieval towns occasionally welcomed kings or other important figures were basically "mumming" on a large scale. In some versions of the Robin Hood myths, the deception of a mummers' procession was used as a ruse to allow the outlaw Merry Men to enter into the royal court undetected.

The tradition of the mummers is also said to have evolved into the modern-day art of pantomime—plays in which actors and actresses use no words, relying rather on body motions and facial expressions to elicit meanings.

ST. VALENTINE'S DAY

ne ancient custom that has survived virtually unchanged in the modern age (no doubt with the aid and blessing of greeting-card manufacturers) is the observance named after St. Valentine, who is believed to have been martyred on February 14, around the year A.D. 271.

People of all ages marked the day by choosing special friends or significant others, affectionately called valentines. This choice was signaled most often by delivering ornate missives, gifts, and various other tokens of affection—typically of an amorous nature, and adorned in bright reds or pinks and heart-shaped icons. Apparently, not a whole lot about the holiday has changed, except for the modern mass production of the gifts themselves.

Also, over the years, the classical deity Cupid—the chubby little cherub whose tiny bow fired darts to pierce the hearts of lovers—worked his way into this romantic tradition.

The holiday was observed primarily in Great Britain, though a similar custom is said to have once prevailed in France, on the first Sunday after the Christian observance of Lent.

The exchange of valentines also appears in a number of literary works, including some by Chaucer and Shakespeare.

Though attributed to the martyred saint, the amorous traditions of St. Valentine's Day may actually have more to do with the old notion that birds began to mate around that time of year.

THE MIRACLE PLAY

iracle plays—or mystery plays, as they were also known—were popular religious performances of the Middle Ages. Though they likely emerged from the often more boisterous traditions of performance enjoyed by pagan cultures, the first miracle plays reportedly took on sacred or religious themes in the wake of the Christianization of ancient pagan societies. This was in keeping with a common evangelical practice of absorbing pagan customs and beliefs into the teachings and rituals of the new faith as, for example, pagan dieties and heroes were associated with Christian saints in certain parts of the world.

Miracle plays were initially performed in churches by members of the clergy. Later acted out in marketplaces by laymen, the subjects of these performances were typically drawn from sacred narratives found in the Old and New Testaments of the Bible. Around the Christmas season, these

The Miracle Plays

plays traditionally dealt with the Nativity, the story of the birth of Jesus Christ in Bethlehem.

In some of the more lavish and grandiose productions, additional platforms above the main stage were occupied by representations of the saints and angels. Stage scenery in these productions often represented various towns, villages, or building fronts. Depending on the stories being performed, some sets even included the entrance to Hell, which was represented by the open mouth of a dragon. These trappings were not altered or taken down from scene to scene. Rather, the scenery was stationary, and it was the actors themselves who moved from place to place as required by the script.

THE LORD
OF MISRULE

he Lord of Misrule—also known as "the Abbot of Unreason" in Scotland—performed the office of "the master of revels" for the kings and great nobles of medieval times during the Christmas season. "The Merry Monarch," as he is called in other sources, is said to have had, for the time being, unlimited power—which was often used to mock the current state of royalty—in leading all the amusements and merriment of the day.

While the tradition of a mock king can also be traced to ancient Rome, some Celtic sources indicate that the reign of "His False Majesty" commenced on All Hallow's Eve (October 31, otherwise known as Halloween) and continued through Candlemas. Candlemas—a Christian festival commemorating the presentation of Christ in the temple and the purification of the Virgin Mary—roughly coincided with Imbolc, the pagan celebration of the first day of spring

(observed on February 1), based on a lunar cycle.

Meanwhile, other sources say the Lord of Misrule's reign lasted only as long as the "Feast of Misrule," over which he presided. The latter seems more likely, as real rulers were not known to forfeit their thrones for extended periods, regardless of tradition. History teaches us that they often had a difficult enough time holding their crowns without such traditions.

Regardless of its duration, it is noted that during his reign, the Lord of Misrule had the entire court at his disposal. Master, as well as all servants of the household, had to obey him. And at this time, servants and master were said to have been on equal terms.

THE MINSTREL

usic has played a role in human existence probably since the first primitive man found pleasure in the simplest of rhythms and melodies—two sticks clacked together, water lapping on a shore, the warbling of a songbird. However, as technologies evolved, so did the art of song and so did its role in human culture.

In primitive societies, music became a vital aspect of ritual and ceremony, and the task of providing aural offerings prbably was shared by various members of society. However, by medieval times, the job of the music maker—or minstrel, as it came to be called—began to take on a more professional nature, with musicians providing their odd talents as a way of earning their keep. In fact, the origin of the word *minstrel* is closely associated with the word *minister*, which means servant.

In the days of England's King Alfred, banquets are said to

have been enlivened by minstrels with harps of three or five strings. In later years troubadours appeared playing the lute, a stringed instrument that some believe was probably borrowed from the Middle East by the Crusaders.

Aside from these professional musicians, knights and their squires also took sport in challenging each other to competitions in music and song. Ballad-singing contests often took place as continuations of tournaments—once all of the jousts and other combats were completed.

However, the art of song was not limited to the warriors, either. It is said that the kings Alfred the Great and Richard I were also accomplished minstrels.

THE SANCTUARY

erived from the Latin word *sanctus*, the word *sanctuary* means "holy." It is also said to have been the source of the English word *saint*. With this in mind, it should not come as a complete surprise that customs outlining this right of protection were closely linked to churches, churchyards, monasteries, and convents.In these religious locations—as well as in various other places—fugitives from justice were safe, as legal or any other violent judgments could not be executed against them there.

In the strictest sense, it was forbidden to inflict harm upon another person in the house or presence of God. It should also be noted, though, that such havens often became prisons, as the protection offered there would evaporate upon the refugees' departure from the sanctuary.

History reports that Robert the Bruce—the famous king who led Scotland to independence in the early 14th

The Sanctuary

century—slew an adversary inside a church and was later excommunicated for his deed by decree of the pope. In England, during the Wars of the Roses, Queen Margaret is said to have taken sanctuary in the Abbey of Beaulieu upon hearing of the defeat of her forces at Barnet.

Though all rights of sanctuary were officially abolished in England in 1623, the concept has never truly died out. Today, however, virtually the only place where the right of sanctuary might be observed is in the embassies of world nations.

ARCHERY
ON THE GREEN

hile it's difficult to say whether archery was developed for hunting or for warfare, it is safe to say that the bow and arrow worked quite well in both arenas. And—under the right conditions—archery was also an enjoyable pastime.

In the hands of ranks of highly skilled archers, the bow and arrow became a fearsome weapon of war, with the potential to devastate an opposing force at great distances. This is particularly true of the English longbow, which matched the archer's height and launched three-foot-long, iron-tipped arrows at targets up to 220 yards away. By law, the best wood was reserved for military bows, but the longbows English civilians used for hunting also proved highly effective in putting food on the table.

In more leisurely times, archery served as a popular sport and archers began to engage in competitions to determine who was the best.

Archery on the Green

654

England is famous for its archers, who were deciding factors in many important early battles. Whether as a result of, or as a contributing factor to, this fame, the sport of archery was also encouraged and regulated by law there. Every person with an annual income of more than 100 pence was required to possess a bow and arrows, and all persons were called upon to practice archery on Sundays and holidays during the hours not occupied by divine service.

THE DUCKING STOOL

machine designed simply to immerse a person in a container or body of water, the ducking stool was little more than a seat at the end of a long wooden pole. It could be as plain or ornate as its builders and users desired, the only features it required being a bit of mobility and a way to secure a person to the seat, as subjects were often less than cooperative.

Though it may look like fun, those put to a soaking thought otherwise, as they were subject to public humiliation and scorn in the best cases. In the worst, those not adept at holding their breath were sometimes lucky to survive the ordeal . . . if they did.

The ducking stool was an engine of punishment for both sexes, and quarrelsome married couples were often immersed back to back. It also wasn't a bad way of sobering drunken rabble-rousers or cooling off brawling louts, though it was also used for punishment of dishonest brewers, bakers,

The Ducking Stool

654

butchers, or any other merchant who sold the public short measure of clothing, foods, or other wares.

The last use of the ducking stool is said to have been at Leominster, England, in 1809. The last *recorded* use, that is.

A modern variation on this theme is a common attraction at many carnivals and fairs in the United States—the "dunking booth." Nowadays, though, a volunteer sits on a plank above a container of water, offering others an opportunity to drop him or her into the drink by hitting a release lever with a thrown ball. It's usually done in the spirit of fun, or to raise money by charging throwers a nominal fee.

THE MAYPOLE

ay Day—or *Beltane*, as it was known by ancient Celts—was one of the most important festivals of the year, ushering in the new life of spring.

Observances of this pagan holiday usually began at midnight on the last day of April. At dawn, the people would hasten into the woods to gather flowers for use as decorations, and also to procure a tall, straight tree. Stripped of its branches, the trunk of this tree would serve as the Maypole.

It was dragged to the village or town, often by as many as 20 or 40 yoke of oxen. There, it was set up and decorated with the gathered flowers and long, flowing ribbons in the widest part of the street or green, to be danced around by the rejoicing people and act as a centerpiece for the festivities.

In some respects, the Maypole represented "the Green Man," a Celtic deity who personified plant life, among other things. The pole, placed upright into the earth, was said to

The Maypole

have been a powerful symbol of fertility. The Celts hoped that if they paid homage to this symbol, all forms of life would flourish and prosper during the coming year.

The traditional dancing—usually in a circle while holding the trailing ribbons that adorned the towering pole—was a symbolic gesture of "raising power," or bolstering the magic in the hewn tree. Circling was another Celtic custom, done counterclockwise (or *deiseal*, which means "sunwise"), in the direction of the sun, thus invoking its power, also.

THE MIDSUMMER
EVE BONFIRE

idsummer Eve was the celebration of the summer solstice, June 21—the day when the sun reaches its highest point in the sky, creating the longest day of the year. In pagan beliefs, the sun god was then at his pinnacle of power. And in his honor, huge bonfires blazed in every town or village as the inhabitants celebrated.

Borrowing somewhat from the traditions observed earlier in the year, at Beltane, these fires were typically staged at high points, such as hilltops, so that they could be seen for miles. The word *bonfire* actually means "bone fire" and was originally a literal description of a fire that was kindled with bones of dead animals.

Assembled around these conflagrations, the people would dance in "sunwise" (counterclockwise) circles and celebrate far into the night. The chief amusement of the young men among them was to jump either over or through

the blaze—hopefully without getting scorched or singed in the process. This is thought by some historians to be the origin of the phrase for being tested, "passing through the fire." Others, however, say the men did it merely to rid themselves of illnesses or ensure health and fertility.

Still other beliefs surrounding this custom are based on some of the rites of the ancient Druids—an enigmatic order of high priests associated with the Celts. The Druids would chant incantations over the fires and then drive village livestock through the blaze in an effort to keep the creatures free of disease.

BRINGING IN THE BOAR'S HEAD

easting over winter holidays was common in early pagan communities. It was assumed among these societies that if food and drink were plentiful during that harsh, cold, and dark time of year, it also would be in good supply during the more hospitable seasons they hoped would soon follow. And as the custom of feasting continued into an era of faith that taught the people that God would provide, so did the aspect of building the feast around a particular dish—roast suckling pig, or boar.

One reason may have been that the pig was a sacred animal among a number of pagan cultures, including Celts, Scandinavians, and Assyrians. Another, more plausible reason may have been that swine were more practical to domesticate and raise in terrain often not suited for larger grazing livestock.

Despite their pagan origins, the feasts carried on into

Bringing in the Boar's Head

Christian tradition, and so did the fare: the first dish brought to the table at the Christmas feasts of old was the boar's head. Tradition has it the boar's head was ushered into the banquet halls with great ceremony, which included the singing of "boar's head carols." It was carried on a grand silver serving dish, garlanded with bay and rosemary.

In most representations, it was also served with an apple stuffed in its mouth. As with the creature itself, the apple was considered a sacred fruit in many pagan cultures. The boar's head dish was also frequently preceded by trumpeters and other musicians, as well as huntsmen carrying boar spears. At the end of the procession came the lowly pages, bearing mustard.

THE WAITS

he waits, obscure groups of roving musicians, are credited by some as being the forerunners of modern-day carolers. Others say they may also have been responsible for the foundation of the English holiday known as Boxing Day.

Originally drawn from the ranks of the watch, the waits eventually came to be known as skilled musicians. Their original repertoire did not include the carols with which they are now associated. Rather, they were known for their musical renditions of old romances and historical legends, such as "Guy of Warwick" and "St. George and the Dragon." Nonetheless, their connection to the Boxing Day holiday stems from their appeals for contributions to their Christmas box—which was, in those days, an actual box created to hold money.

Celebrated in Great Britain, Canada, and Australia, Boxing Day is customarily held on December 26. The tradition

The Waits

dates to a Middle Ages practice of opening the church's "poor box" for the purpose of distributing its contents among the needy of the town.

Another later custom associated with this observance was the giving of money—again, in a box, although smaller—to those who had given service during the year, such as postmen, delivery men, and household servants.

Though Boxing Day never actually caught on in the United States, Americans have more or less invented a custom of their own that loosely fits the name "Boxing Day," if not the spirit—returning boxes of ill-chosen gifts to stores.

THE JESTER

elegated to the lowly status of images on playing cards today, jesters were once important members of medieval households. Also known as jokers, it was their duty to keep the spirits of their lords and ladies high.

The need for such a role may have stemmed from a growing cultural diversity. In the days when the art of polite conversation was not a common virtue among most members of so-called polite society, it was jesters who amused guests during any awkward silences encountered during feasts and other social occasions. Because many of these events were attended by armed warriors, a cloud of foul humor caused by a clash of customs or beliefs could, and sometimes did, lead to bloodshed.

Because of their office, jesters were typically granted the privilege of poking fun at anyone in the house, regardless of his or her standing. As a result, if they were good at their

vocations, they were usually able to keep the hall in an uproar of merriment.

Though often depicted as fools and dolts, jesters were often more intelligent than many in their company. They had to be—insulting the wrong person at the wrong time could prove disastrous. They often wisely focused their humor on the ones the king liked least, or opted to poke fun at themselves.

Like many modern-day clowns or comedians, jesters often took their humor to vivid extremes, adorning themselves in outlandish and often ridiculous costumes with bells and other garish forms of exaggeration.

THE TOURNAMENT
(TRIAL BY COMBAT)

T he tournament was one of the grandest and most identifying spectacles of medieval society, and it is within such settings that many classic tales of knights and chivalry were cast—including the legend of King Arthur and his Knights of the Round Table, as well as the opening chapters of Sir Walter Scott's famous literary work, *Ivanhoe*.

The main event of a medieval tournament was frequently a joust, in which participants wielded headless lances that most often resulted in nothing more serious than a few bruises or broken ribs. There were strict rules for these events, where honor was more often at stake than life. And while winners could claim prizes ranging from gold to a maiden's hand in marriage, losers were likely to earn the contempt of the kingdom.

Combat, however, was far more serious—and usually deadly. Combat was often the means of settling legal quarrels,

The Journament 654

such as charges of high treason. In combat, a ring or glove of challenge was given and received, and a day of trial appointed. Accuser and accused would then meet in "the lists"—an arena that usually was 60 paces long and 40 paces wide. There, they fought to the finish—usually beginning on horseback with spears, then with swords, and finally, concluding the combat on foot with daggers.

The victor of combat was then declared to be in the right, or vindicated. As for the loser, he was condemned, or determined wrong, and if he was still alive at the end, it typically wasn't for long. If the wounds he sustained weren't fatal enough on their own, he was usually executed.

THE SCOTTISH FIERY CROSS

A tradition hailing from Scotland, the "Fiery Cross," as it came to be called, was used by the Highland chiefs as a summons for the rapid assembling of their respective clans.

According to Highland clan lore, each clan had a special gathering place where its members would assemble in times of emergency. When the Fiery Cross was passed, Highland warriors knew they were to take up arms and hurry to these congregation sites to await news of the crisis and receive their orders from their chieftain.

Though the symbol itself consisted of a stick of wood, it was not necessarily fashioned in the form of a cross. However, in pagan tradition, the stick was commonly charred in fire and then dipped in the blood of a slaughtered animal. And most often, the dire icon was carried by a pair of messengers who would run through the clan's territories shouting their rousing military mottoes or slogans.

The (Scottish) Fiery Cross

As clan territories were often quite extensive, Fiery Crosses were typically relayed by a series of messengers.

A modern adaptation of this old practice was seen in the famous midnight ride of Paul Revere at the dawn of America's Revolutionary War in 1775. On horseback, Revere is said to have galloped tirelessly through the towns around Boston, Massachusetts, to warn colonial minutemen of the arrival of British troops.

OAK APPLE DAY

With a little effort, the somewhat obscure old custom of "Oak Apple Day" can be traced to none other than Prince Charles II of the Stuart family of kings of Scotland and England.

In the tumultuous times that led up to the first of the Jacobite uprisings in Scotland, his father, Charles I, was executed in 1649 by English forces. Fearful of a similar fate, Charles II fled to France.

In 1651, with sufficient support for his cause regenerated, he returned and claimed the Scottish throne. However, when he attempted to take the throne of England, he met with defeat at the hands of Lord Protector Oliver Cromwell at the Battle of Worcester, and once again headed for France—to "go about his travels," it was said.

The tradition of Oak Apple Day reportedly emerged from a strange event that occurred during this second flight. Charles II is said to have spent an entire day hiding in an oak

ak Apple Day.

tree to await the cover of darkness to continue his retreat. Legend has it that he was provided with a pillow and a smattering of food and the locals of the region gathered near the hideout to advise him of danger. And though considerable reward was offered for his apprehension, none betrayed him, and he eventually reached safety in France.

In 1660, following Cromwell's death, Charles II finally took the English throne in what was called the Stuart Restoration. Later, it was ordered that his birthday (May 29) be kept as a "perpetual anniversary with thanksgiving." The wearing of acorns (oak apples) became customary on that day in celebration of his grand escape to France.

THE STOCKS

 common site in historical representations of old-time jails in the United States, the stocks originated in England, probably during the reign of Edward III. They were used primarily for punishing vagrants, beggars, and other generally disorderly people.

The physical function of these stocks, of course, was the restriction of movement, and thereby, freedom. But the psychological effects upon the offender were far more important. Because the stocks stood in highly visible public places, the offender was subject to public humiliation—which, it was hoped, would shame him or her into reforming.

The image most often brought to mind at the mention of stocks is of a hunched-over wrongdoer in a semistanding position with hands and head restrained by heavy blocks of wood. However, this describes a more "modern" version of the stocks, which is technically called the pillory and which

Puritans brought to the colonies in North America. Older versions, used in England, were designed so the offender would be seated.

With their feet securely held in strong wooden frames, the culprits were compelled to sit while they were exposed to the ridicule and taunting of the local loafers—or any other upstanding citizens who happened to pass by. In fact, this type of punishment by humiliation may well have contributed in some way to the coining of the term "upstanding citizen"—as those who weren't bound and seated in stocks truly could be called upstanding citizens.

CURING THE "KING'S EVIL"

rior to modern advances in the medical arts, many ordinary diseases were elevated to supernatural status and were likewise treated with equally unearthly cures. But even beyond the ages of superstition, the "King's Evil," as it was called, was previously thought to have been a disease of defective nutrition, caused by insufficient dietary intake.

Nowadays, it is known as scrofula, a form of tuberculosis that attacks the lymph nodes of the neck. And it has since been learned that the disease was caused by drinking milk that had become infected with harmful bacteria.

The disease's name of old, the King's Evil, stemmed from the belief that the touch of a king could heal a sufferer. In England, it is said that Edward the Confessor was the first to "touch for the Evil," an act for which there appeared a special "healing service" in the prayer book of Henry VIII. Queen Anne is credited as the last sovereign to "touch for

Curing the "King's Evil"

the Evil" (in 1712), with one of her "patients" being the famous author and lexicographer Dr. Samuel Johnson.

Nonetheless, it is highly doubtful that anyone in those days ever actually cured anything with a mere touch or a prayer. Treatment today—even with the miracles of 20th-century medical technology—includes antituberculous chemotherapy.

Though the incidence of scrofula has been greatly reduced in recent years through eradication of the disease in dairy cattle and modern pasteurization techniques, tuberculosis kills some 3 million people each year worldwide. In the United States, the death rate from TB is in the neighborhood of 1 in every 30,000.

"A DISH OF TEA"

ea may be synonymous with British society today, but that wasn't always the case. And Great Britain was not among the first cultures to know the pleasures of this bitter but delightful herb.

Though often associated with the Orient, tea actually originated in India. From there, the plant was first introduced in China around A.D. 500 Later, around 793, the first known tax on the substance was levied in China. It wasn't until 1191 that tea was first introduced to Japan, where the drinking of tea was later banned in 1350.

Two and a half centuries later, tea from China was first shipped to Europe, by the Dutch East India Company in 1609. It took nearly another 30 years, but by 1636, tea made its debut in Paris.

The first cup of tea was reportedly not brewed in England until 1650, the same year Britain's first coffeehouse

A Dish of Tea

opened at Oxford. Following its introduction, tea—which was also known as "tay," or "tee"—remained something of a rarity in England for nearly the next four decades. It wasn't until around 1689 that "a spot of tea" finally became prevalent in England.

CALLING THE HOURS
(THE WATCHMAN)

Before there were police forces, the duty of keeping order in growing communities often belonged to a group of men known collectively as "the watch." Initially the watch may have been an efficient force, but the members of these units frequently degenerated into a lazy and less-than-honest lot that came to be known as "the Charlies." In this incarnation, they were usually described as crusty old men who preferred taking in the cozy atmosphere of the local ale houses to performing their appointed duties.

One of those duties involved parading the streets and "calling the hours." Accompanying this oral report—which was shouted from various locales around the town—was also the state of the weather and other affairs. Thus came phrases like, "Eleven o'clock and all's well."

In Scotland, another type of watch emerged. Called "the Black Watch," it earned a reputation, according to some, as

Calling the Hour

being no better than the outlaw element it was designed to control. In *Manners, Customs and History of the Highlanders of Scotland*, Sir Walter Scott wrote that these independent companies were raised to repress disturbances and were deemed "a remedy of doubtful and dangerous character."

According to Scott, and others, the Black Watch often helped themselves to whatever loot they obtained from the thieves they apprehended. Nonetheless, some assert that this was still a small price to pay for the peace that was kept as a result of their presence.

THE DUEL

he duel appears to have been a natural progression of the ancient "trial by combat."

Even though societies became more civilized, and even though citizens no longer toted around battlefield broadswords, it was still an accepted practice for gentlemen to wear equally lethal rapiers at their sides. And, then as now, disagreements between citizens erupted with some regularity.

It should come as no great surprise that, under such conditions, duels were a frequent occurrence, most often fought on the spot of the disputes that triggered them. During England's Elizabethan period, rapiers reportedly became so long, and their owners so reckless, that the length of the weapon was strictly limited by law. Officials were empowered to break off any length that exceeded the legal limit.

As the wearing of swords gradually died out, their place in the custom of the duel was eventually taken by pistols.

The Duel.

Under a variety of rules, combatants would typically fire upon each other on the word of command agreed upon prior to the deadly exchange. Physicians were typically found in attendance at duels.

Undertakers weren't far in the background either, as, with such advancements in killing technologies, someone was likely to die. And with the introduction of firearms, the chances increased that a participant in a duel would share a cemetery residence with his opponent.

THE OLD TIME BANK
(THE GOLDSMITH'S CHEST)

hile today funds are moved in and out of our bank accounts electronically, and credit cards and checks make it possible to purchase the necessities of life without using currency, keeping one's money physically secure was once a major concern.

Long before the modern practices of banking emerged, merchants in England committed their hard-earned money to the trusted custody of the Royal Mint, located "securely" in the Tower of London.

At least that was the case until King Charles I arbitrarily seized a sizeable amount of this deposit in the early 1600s. So, safer custodians were sought and found in, of all places, goldsmiths. These fine craftsmen were said to have kept their receipts in marvelously constructed iron-bound chests— most of which were secured with complex locking mechanisms. By this means, early goldsmiths gradually rose from

mere artificers to become wealthy and influential bankers.

There are several reasons why this custom was successful for a time. One is that the intricately designed locking mechanisms rendered these chests nearly impregnable. Another is that gold, being a dense and heavy metal, presented thieves with a "weighty" problem—the trunks themselves were simply too heavy to haul off without fear of being detected or caught in a slow flight.

Whatever the reasons, the practice still seems better than using a mattress or a cookie jar.

CHRONOLOGY
A Time Line of Selected Ancient and Annual Customs

1000–1 B.C. – Professional musicians perform at ceremonies in Isreal; Celts move into England and Celtic settlements appear elsewhere in British Isles; the first public combats between gladiators are held in Rome.

A.D. 1–500 – Romans invade Britain; the Christian faith is born; St. Valentine martyred; Romans driven out of British Isles; St. Patrick begins missions to Ireland.

501–1000 – England divides into shires, and castles become seats of European nobility; Irish missionary St. Columba establishes monastery on Scottish island Iona; Christianity spreads through British Isles; fear of the end of the world is widespread.

1001–1100 – Introduction of "curfew bell" into English tradition by William the Conqueror, duke of Normandy, named first Norman king of England in 1066; Edward the Confessor first to "touch" for the "King's Evil."

1101–1300 – English knights participate in tournaments to test their skills and bravery; under English law, the best wood is reserved to make longbows, and archery is practiced by all men; minstrels travel the countryside, performing for nobles and knights; Miracle plays, or mystery plays, are performed in English towns.

1301–1700 – The stocks are introduced as a form of punishment in England; Charles I helps himself to funds in the Royal Mint; Tea is introduced in England; Oak Apple Day proclaimed; rights of sanctuary abolished.

1701–1800 – The "King's Evil" is "cured" by Queen Anne; a "Fiery Cross" is used to raise clans in Jacobite risings in the Highlands of Scotland.

INDEX

Further Reading

Chadwick, Nora. *The Celts*. New York: Penguin Books Ltd., 1991.

Ferguson, Diana. *The Magickal Year: A Pagan Perspective on the Natural World*. New York: Quality Paperback Book Club, 1996.

Grun, Bernard. *The Timetables of History*. New York: Simon & Schuster/Touchstone, 1991.

Lorie, Peter. *Superstitions*. New York: Simon & Schuster, 1992.

Matthews, Caitlin. *The Celtic Book of Days: A Guide to Celtic Spirituality & Wisdom*. Rochester, Vermont: Destiny Books, 1995.

Powers, Mala. *Follow the Year: A Family Celebration of Christian Holidays*. San Francisco: Harper & Row Publishers Inc., 1985.

Ross, Anne. *Folklore of the Scottish Highlands*. New York: Barnes & Noble Books Inc., 1993.

Scott, Sir Walter. *Manners, Customs and History of the Highlanders of Scotland*. New York: Barnes & Noble Books Inc., 1993.

Stewart, Bob, and John Matthews. *Legendary Britain: An Illustrated Journey*. London: Blanford Press, 1992.